Foluke Ogunleye obtained her PhD in Theatre Arts from the University of Ibadan. An Actress and Director, she formed her Theatre Company; Christian Multimedia International (formerly Christian Theatre Studio) in 1990. Her published plays include *The Broken Hedge* (2002), *The Innocent Victim* (2003), A *Little Attack of Pregnancy* (2003), *Mothers, Sisters and Daughters* (2003). She has written many books and journal articles in the areas of Theatre and Media Studies. She currently teaches Drama in the Department of African Languages and Literature at the University of Swaziland, Kwaluseni, Swaziland.

BY THE SAME AUTHOR

PUBLISHED PLAYS
Nest in a Cage (1997)
The Broken Hedge (2002)
The Innocent Victim (2003)
A Little Attack of Pregnancy (2003)
Mothers. Sisters and Daughters (2003)

FILMS PRODUCED
The Solid Rock (1993)
Supermender (1994)
The Visit (1994)
The Returns (1994)
Two in One (1994)
The Broken Hedge (1997)
Abiye (1999)
Born to Live (2000)

PLAYS PERFORMED BUT NOT YET PUBLISHED
10:10 Connection (1986)
Born to Live (1987)
In His Steps (1988)
Noah's Ark (1989)
Hurdles (1989)

Foluke Ogunleye

NEST IN A CAGE

TTI Publishing Ltd
Manzini, Swaziland

First published in Nigeria in 1997 by Linnet Paul Publications
This edition first published in Swaziland in 2004 by TTI Publishing (Pty) Ltd.
P. O. Box 7093, Manzini M200, Swaziland
tti.publications@webmail.co.za

ISBN   0-7978-0002-6

INTRODUCTION

For a very long time in the Nigerian theatre, the pen has been mostly in the hands of men. Consequently, the image of women portrayed in Nigerian dramatic literature has often been one-sided. Although Nigeria has not been totally bereft of female playwrights, the number of women who pursue the histrionic arts- especially from the 'writing' point of view- has certainly been much less than the men. However, the story is changing for the better. More female playwrights are emerging and we are seeing stories of women being told from a woman's point of view. One of such stories is *Nest in a Cage*.

Nest in a Cage can be described as a modern morality play. It debunks the myth among many modern young girls that material success can only be attained through consorting with debauched rich old men. This myth has been fostered through patriarchal social structures, which has ensured that riches are mostly in the hands of men, and also, the patriarchal fallacy of the polygamous instinct, which allows men, no matter how old, to seek adulterous trysts with girls young enough to be their daughters. These two factors place the old men in positions of undue advantage - they lure the girls and lead them astray with their filthy lucre and also use the excuse of polygamy to exploit and discard them at will.

The play also warns that living a morally loose life can only lead to calamity. The play examines the evils of abortion and graphically presents the troubles that emanate from the act. According to the play, abortion is mostly perpetrated when irresponsible men shirk their duties towards the poor girls they impregnate. Finally, the play shows that hard work and determination are the ways out of slavish dependency on the male for sustenance. The story is essentially told through flashback. Dr. (Mrs.) Nike Adagunodo, a medical doctor of great repute, has been invited to address a group of secondary school girls about good behavior. However, in true adolescent spirit, one of the students challenges her to talk about her past.

'Writing women' has been universally acclaimed as an important exercise the world over. As a matter of fact, women's issues have attained the front burner internationally. For example, the United Nation's Decade for Women, Equality, Development and Peace acknowledged the import of women in development, also, the Nairobi Forward Looking Strategies (NFLS) emphasized the need for effective integration of women into the development process. This play is a step in that same direction.

Nest in a Cage parades for us a bevy of ladies – the good, the bad and the ugly. We see those who contribute their own quota to make the society better. They make their presence felt in a positive way. We also see the ones who strive to destroy others of their type in order to realize their own personal selfish ambition. In summation, the fact that the women are good or bad provides a message for the audience. It makes a statement also that women are not 'invisible' in society. They maintain a presence, which is very important. We see them, not as stereotypical models as we see in the patriarchal plays – women as décor, prostitutes, low-income workers etc., but as sturdy characters who exist in the typical day-to-day life of the average Nigerian.

Foluke Ogunleye, Ph.D.
Swaziland, 2004

Characters

PRINCIPAL	Of Paragon Girls' College
FIRST TEACHER	Teacher at Paragon Girls' College
TEACHER II	Teacher at Paragon Girls' College
BUSOLA	Student at Paragon Girls' College
STUDENTS	Of Paragon Girls' College
LANRE	University undergraduate
DEOLA	University undergraduate
NIKE	Fresher at the University
FATHER	Nike's Father
MOTHER	Nike's Mother
DUPE	Medical Student and Nike's friend
CHIEF AGBABIAKA	Nike's Sugar Daddy
MRS. AGBABIAKA	His wife
DOCTOR DAGUNDURO	Agbabiaka's family Doctor
TAYO JACKSON	Nike's friend
NEIGHBOR	Nike's neighbor
FRIEND	Nike's friend

Nest in a Cage was produced on the 1st and 2nd of April 2004 at the University of Swaziland, Kwaluseni, Swaziland with the following cast and crew, and with Swazi names:

Cast

PRINCIPAL	Sindisiwe Dlamini
FIRST TEACHER	Thandazile Shabalala
SECOND TEACHER	Mkhaliphi Cynthia
BUSOLA (ZINHLE SHIBA)	Nqobile Shongwe
LANRE (NOMSA)	Fortunate Zwane
DEOLA (THEMBI)	Nel'siwe Gama
NIKE (ZANDI)	Nompumelelo Dladla
	Khosi Mahlalela

FATHER	Lucky Mabuza
	Nkosiyomusa Dlamini
MOTHER	Rebecca Masilela
	Sindi Nkambule
DUPE (THABSILE)	Sindi Tsela
CHIEF AGBABIAKA (SIMELANE)	Sifiso Hlanze
MRS. AGBABIAKA (SIMELANE'S WIFE)	Mumcy Shoba
DOCTOR DAGUNDURO (MABUZA)	Mphicwa M. Dlamini
TAYO JACKSON (MICHAEL SMITH)	Ntsikelelo Dlamini
FRIEND	Sithungo Ceb'sile

STUDENTS/CHORUS:

Dlamini Dumsile	Dlamini Gab'sile
Dlamini Manqoba	Dlamini Nkosiyomusa
Dlamini Nonhlanhla	Dlamini Philile
Dubase Ntokozo	Gumbi Lungile
Hlatshwako Futhi	Khumalo Themb'sile
Kunene Dalton	Kunene Florence
Matse Khanyile	Mhlanga Duma
Ngwenya Samu	Nxumalo Lindokuhle
Sithungo Ceb'sile	Vilakati Bongani
Zishwili Zethu	Zwane Zanele

Business/Box office Manager	Thulani Maseko
Compugraphy	Ntokozo Dubase
Costume/Make-Up	Zanele Zwane
	Zethu Zishwili
	Florence Kunene
	Lindokuhle Nxumalo
Lighting	Duma Mhlanga
Prompter	Victor Dlamini
Publicity	Sithungo Ceb'sile
	Dlamini Gab'sile
Set Construction	Duma Mhlanga
	Queen Nhlekoh
Sound	Melusi Khanyile
Stage Manager	Bongani Bulunga

Playwright/Director's Note for the University of Swaziland Production

In this modern world, bereft of morals, abortion and 'sugar daddyism' have become orders of the day. These also walk hand in hand with the dreaded HIV/AIDS pandemic. This play, *Nest in a Cage* addresses the issues mentioned above, and recommends a moral rearmament in modern society. Seeing that 'the hand that rocks the cradle rules the world', this play recommends the empowerment of the girl-child- spiritually, morally and educationally. This seems to be the only hope for humanity.

The maiden performance of *Nest in a Cage* took place at Obafemi Awolowo University, Ile-Ife, Nigeria in 1997. This second performance is coming across many lands. The characters' names and locales have been adapted to suit Swazi culture, but the spirit remains the same. This play is my humble sacrifice to make the world a better place. May God accept the sacrifice of love.

Foluke Ogunleye, Ph.D.
Kwaluseni, Swaziland, 2004

PROLOGUE

The assembly hall of Paragon Girls' College. The roll is being called by one of the teachers. The Principal is pacing up and down behind her. Other teachers are seated. The students may either be seated in the first few rows in the auditorium or in the gallery, if there is one.

TEACHER: Titilawo Morounkeji.

STUDENT: Present ma.

TEACHER: Uwandu Grace.

STUDENT: Present ma.

TEACHER: Williams Titilayo.

STUDENT: Present ma.

TEACHER: Yesufu Hannatu.

STUDENT: Present ma.

TEACHER: Yusuf Busola (no response. P*ause*). Yusuf Busola (*turns to Principal*). Madam, one of the girls is missing.

PRINCIPAL: (s*napping to attention*). Missing? Which one of them?

TEACHER: Yusuf Busola, madam.

PRINCIPAL: Oh, not that problem girl again! Where on earth could she have disappeared to? I hope I will not lose my job because of this idiot of a girl.

TEACHER II: But madam, you sent her to the detention room for jumping the fence to attend a party in town last night.

PRINCIPAL: Oh, is she still there? Please hurry up and bring her here.

TEACHER II: All right madam (s*he goes*).

PRINCIPAL: I hope this girl will not bring about my death in this school. I wonder why she is always so irascible. After all, she is not the only one from a broken home.

TEACHER: She seems to be so angry at the whole world and so determined to hurt everybody in sight.

PRINCIPAL: It is a great pity. She has so much potential, but she is suffering from a sense of defeat.

TEACHER: Her father has convinced her that because her mother ran away with another man while she was still a baby, nobody could possibly love her and that she cannot make any headway in life.

PRINCIPAL: It is a great pity. She seems to seek for solace in the arms of boys.

TEACHER: She is morally bankrupt.

PRINCIPAL: Well, finish the roll call and let's get on with other things.

TEACHER: Zacheus Taiwo.

STUDENT: Present ma.

TEACHER: Zacheus Kehinde

STUDENT: Present ma.

TEACHER: (*turns to the Principal*). That's all madam. They are all accounted for (*sits down*).

PRINCIPAL: Good (*walks to the rostrum*). Good afternoon girls.

STUDENT: Good afternoon ma.

PRINCIPAL: The day has finally come, a special day for Paragon Girls' College. For some weeks now, we have been announcing to you that the patroness of our school, Dr. (Mrs.) Nike Adagunodo will be here today to give us a talk (*second teacher enters with Busola*).

TEACHER II: Here she is madam.

PRINCIPAL: Oh, there you are. I hope the punishment you have been through will bring you to your senses. Why must you always be running after boys? They will just wreck your life and leave you to fend for yourself. I thought of leaving you in the detention room, but I just felt you might be able to gain a thing or two from our patroness. Now sit right here in front of me in the first row where I can keep my eyes on you. I'll see how you can get into mischief here.

BUSOLA: (*she had been looking at the principal with an expression of disdain. She finally moves to the indicated seat with defiance*). Yes ma.

PRINCIPAL: (*Principal continues with her speech*). As I was saying girls, Dr. (Mrs.) Adagunodo is coming today and I will implore you to be very quiet and of good behavior. Who knows, she might just decide to hand out a couple of scholarships while she is here. Do not forget the order of the programme that we have gone through with you many times before. Immediately she enters. You will … (*She is interrupted by the sound of a car*). Oh my God, that must be Dr.

2

(Mrs.) Adagunodo now (*she rushes outside and the teachers follow her*).

BUSOLA: (*bursts into laughter and climbs the stage*). Oh my! What a pack of sycophants (*mimicking the principal*). Dr. (Mrs.) Adagunodo this, Dr. (Mrs.) Adagunodo that! Ah, you would think she must be God himself. What is this hullabaloo about the stupid woman? Is she not a human being like the rest of us? You would think she doesn't go to the toilet like us lesser human beings. I am sure she must be one ugly looking old woman who was lucky enough to have become maybe the 'number ten' or 'number twenty' wife of a stupid old man who must have embezzled our money and then bought herself an honorary doctorate degree. That is what they always do. You will see, we will all be bored to death. But don't you worry; I will give her a tough time. I'm sure somebody must have written the speech for her. Bloody illiterate.

She runs back to her seat as the entourage files in. The Principal in front, followed by Dr. (Mrs.) Adagunodo and the teachers. As they enter, the girls stand up and remain standing until the guest of honor is seated.

PRINCIPAL: You are very much welcome to our school madam. Thank you very much for doing us this honor. The students will now present the special songs and dances, which they have been preparing to honor you with on this august occasion (*different groups of girls come forward to present songs and dances*).

SONG: Adenike kaabo
Paragon ku Ile
A ki o o, Adenike
Aya Adagunodo
Aya rere l'odede oko re
Afinju onisegun ti i wo igba arun
Adenike a ki o o
Owo ide, ese ide
Adenike rora rin iwo l'oju gbogbo n' wo
Ma rora rin iwo l'oju gbogbo n' wo
Aya Adagunodo rora rin iwo l'oju gbogbo n' wo
Ma rora rin iwo l'oju gbogbo n' wo

Adenike rora rin
Omo gbajumo, aya gbajumo, iwo gaangaan, gbajumo
Ko s'olosi n'iran re
Olowo, olowo, olowo ni gbogbo ebi re
Ero ya, e wa w'ere
Ero ya, e wa wo'ran
Ero to n'lo, e wa w'ere, e wa woran
Ero ya, e wa wo'ran
Ta lo ko wa jo sibi?
Nike Adagunodo ni
Tori taa la se pejo sibi?
Nike Adagunodo ni
Waa ko wa je pe, aya Adagunodo
Ki lo n'dun loju orun?
Mo wo'ke rere mo ri baluu kan
Nike Adagunodo lo fi baluu se'ese rin
Ese ide ko see fi wo'doti
Nike Adagunodo
Maa wo'le, maa rora
Wo'le ni baba alejo
E kaabo o.[1]

PRINCIPAL: Thank you very much girls. That was very nice. It is now time for us to listen to the much-awaited talk. It is with great pleasure that I present to you our much-honored patroness, who has agreed to do us this great honor by finding time out of her very busy schedule to address us. Please put your hands together and welcome Dr. (Mrs.) Nike Adagunodo (*everybody claps as she comes forward*).

ADAGUNODO: Thank you very much ladies. It is indeed a great pleasure for me to be here with you today. The title of my speech is *Keep Yourself Pure*. When I see your beautiful, bright and hopeful faces, I remember what I used to be at your age, full of hope and feeling that the world was at my feet. The sky is your limit dear children. You can have whatever you desire. But there is a thief. There is a thief that desires to steal your ambition and your opportunities. The thief wants to steal your talents, your potentials and your abilities. The thief does not come like an armed robber, coming to rob you with force; otherwise, you'll be able to defend yourself. He comes in

4

disguise. Not just one, he has many disguises. For example, he may decide to come in the disguise of your friends, encouraging you to go into various vices (*she goes into the audience and brings one girl out*). "Oh, you mean you have never smoked before? Ah, you must try this. Just one puff and if you don't like it, you may stop" (*she releases the girl to go and sit down*). But that one puff is the road to addiction (*she goes into the audience and brings another girl out*). "You want to stay awake at night to read? Why don't you try this powder? It is simply wonderful!" (*she releases the girl to go and sit down*). Well my girl, you just try it and you will be on your way to drug addiction (*she goes into the audience and brings a third girl out*). "You mean you are still a virgin? Oh what an outdated prude you are! You must move with the times girl (*whispers conspiratorially*). You see that guy over there? He is my boyfriend's bosom friend. He's been dying for you in secret. He said I should talk to you about him? He wants you to accompany us to a party tonight. Will you come along? He really loves you very much and can actually die for you. You know I will never deceive you" (*she releases the girl to go and sit down*). That is a lie. She is not your friend. She only wants to spoil your life. Why don't you face your studies and keep yourself pure. Those boys will wreck your life and leave you to face your problems alone. If you fail your exams, you will become a liability to them. If you contact sexually transmitted diseases, they will run from you ...

BUSOLA: (*springs up*). Shit, I can't stand this anymore. How dare you pretend to us that you are a saint? You want to tell me that you did not play the field in your bad old days? I am sure you sampled quite a lot of dudes before landing the rich old guy you eventually married. Do you want to tell me that you found him in the corner of your room where you were dutifully reading your books and keeping yourself pure?

PRINCIPAL: (*shocked*). Busola Yusuf! Have you gone mad? (*moves to her and pushes her roughly*)Will you walk out of this auditorium and go back to the detention room from where you've just been released?

ADAGUNODO: (*places herself between the two*). Oh no, please leave her alone. I am sure she is genuinely curious about me (*she steers the principal back to her seat and turns to Busola, placing her hands on her shoulder*). You are right my girl, I wasn't always like this. I had to learn my lesson the hard way. That is why I have come to you today, to turn you from the path of hardship and suffering that I trod, to encourage and empower you to make the best use of the opportunities that life may have given you (*she motions to Busola to return to her seat*). You see, I grew up in a very humble home. My parents were very poor, and I grew up lacking most of the good things of life. I finished my secondary school in the village. I was quite innocent. The village life used to be a very sheltered one in those days. But then, I couldn't stay there forever; I gained admission into a university in the city.

The play moves into flashback mode.

Lights Fade Out

PART ONE

Scene 1

A university female hostel room with four beds. Two girls are in the room setting up their individual corners and conversing.

LANRE: It's sure nice to be back in school after the long vac. The holiday was a big bore.

DEOLA: Really? My own vacation was quite thrilling. I had a wonderful time. Actually, I was hoping something would happen, like our lecturers going on strike, students doing aluta[2], or the whole country going on Anti-SAP riots[3] again so that our holidays would be extended.

LANRE: Ah, lucky you. I am sure I would have gone mad if the holidays had been extended. You see, my parents are so conservative. They didn't allow me to live the kind of life I lived on campus. I had to stay at home throughout, no parties, and the boys that were coming to cheer me up, my father scared them all away. He even threatened to beat me up one day. The old man does not realize that I'm no longer a baby. I am now in part three and soon, I'll be a graduate. Still, he wanted to beat me up!

DEOLA: You don't say! I can't take that kind of nonsense from anybody. Anyway, my parents do not have time for me; neither do I have time for them. My father is always engrossed in one board meeting or another when he is in the country. Most of the time, he is away on business trips.

LANRE: Aren't you lucky! But what of your mother?

DEOLA: My mother? (*laughs*). She is like a doctor's prescription.

LANRE: A doctor's prescription? What do you mean?

DEOLA: She goes to her shop first thing in the morning and returns last thing at night (*they both laugh*).

LANRE: Indeed!

DEOLA: There is no love lost between us anyway. She cares only for my senior brother and I don't give a damn about them all.

LANRE: That means you must have been left on your own all the time. Wasn't it boring?

DEOLA: (laughs). Boring? Boring my foot! I always waited patiently until they all left the house and then went on my own merry way. You know I made a lot of friends last session. I had a rosy time with them during the break.

LANRE: (*moves over to Deola's* corner). Lucky girl. Gist me about the rosy times.

DEOLA: Are you sure you will not be envious? (*laughs*). Anyway, you know I had this torrid affair going with Alhaji Maikudi before we left the campus?

LANRE: Yes I remember he was head over heels in love with you before we went home.

DEOLA: Well, he had to travel to the United States for two weeks and he said he couldn't live for two full weeks without me. So, to save his blood pressure, I decided to go with him.

LANRE: Two weeks in America? What did you tell your parents?

DEOLA: I simply waited till they were out of the house and dropped a note that I would be with one of my girl friends for the next two weeks and that was all.

LANRE: (*wistfully*). Some girls have all the luck in the world.

DEOLA: I had an almost embarrassing experience when I was in America.

LANRE: What happened?

DEOLA: Three days before we were to return home, Alhaji decided to take me a-shopping. We were in a large dress shop when I looked down the aisle and who did I see?

LANRE: Who?

DEOLA: It was no other person than my father coming 'down the aisle', literally and figuratively, with a young girl, about my age, clinging to his arm like a life support system.

LANRE: Wao! Are you kidding?

DEOLA: The girl was obviously his girlfriend and he was buying her all sorts of expensive things. Things he would never buy for his own children. Anyway, I quickly ducked inside a changing room and stayed there till they left.

LANRE: Poor you. It would have been a real sticky thing if you had come face to face. But Alhaji must really love you to be spending so much money on you. Are you planning to marry him?

DEOLA: You are still new in this business. Money means nothing to him. Can you believe that since we came back from the US, I have not seen him?

LANRE: Why?

DEOLA: He hasn't been taking my calls. His secretary always tells me he's out. But I know it's his way of telling me it's over. That was the way he treated the girl he had before me.

LANRE: Oh, that is rather bad.

DEOLA: Anyway, I am not wasting any sweat on him. I met another man at a party a few days after the US trip. He is a Managing Director of a big company in Lagos. Actually we are going out together tonight.

LANRE: What of your boyfriend in Russia?

DEOLA: Oh Depo? Well, I make sure I write him faithfully every week: (*in an exaggerated declamatory manner*)"My Darling Depo, you are the only sugar in my tea, the only mosquito in my net, the only cockroach in my cupboard... etc." (*laughs*). However, I am sure he is enjoying himself with Russian girls too, so why should I starve myself?

LANRE: This party of yours tonight, is it an exclusive thing or can gatecrashers tag along? I am bored stiff. You know my boyfriend has graduated now and I have lost touch with all the 'bobo nice'⁴ that I acquired last session.

DEOLA: Oh yes, Tola is serving⁵ now. Where has he been posted to?

LANRE: He is serving in Kaduna State.

DEOLA: All right then, I'd better take pity on you and take you along. I daresay we can get you a boyfriend before the night is over.

LANRE: Oh come off it. I don't need a boyfriend. I just want to enjoy myself. I want to find out whether I still know how to dance after almost three months of monastery life in my father's house (*they both laugh. Lanre plays some music on the tape. They both start dancing until somebody knocks on the door. Lanre responds*). Come in.

DEOLA: If you are good looking and rich, that is.

A middle-aged couple with poverty written all over them enter with their teenaged daughter.

FATHER: (*hesitant*). Good afternoon my girls. I am neither good looking nor rich, but my daughter has been allocated to this room.

LANRE: Good afternoon sir. Please don't mind our little joke. That will be her bed (*she points to the only bed that is not yet laid*).

DEOLA: (*addressing the young girl*). Oh, you are our Jambite[6]? You are very welcome. I wish you a wonderful stay on this campus.

MOTHER: Thank you my daughters. You don't know how much relief it gives my heart to know that my daughter will be living in the same room with nice, beautiful girls like you. Please, she has never traveled out of the village before. This is her first time of coming to the city. Help me look after her.

LANRE: Ah. Don't worry ma. We will look after her.

FATHER: How long have you been in the university?

DEOLA: This is our third year.

FATHER: That is very good. What are you studying?

DEOLA: We are in the social sciences.

FATHER: I see. My daughter has been admitted through direct entry to study medicine. Her name is Nike Adedara. I am Mr. Adedara. I am the headmaster of the only primary school in our village. This is Mrs. Adedara, my worthy wife. She is a sewing mistress. You shall be seeing us here quite frequently. Like her mother said, this is Nike's first trip out of the village, and it is the first night she will spend away from home. Please, you are older than her; help us to keep an eye on her.

LANRE: We will sir.

FATHER: Thank you very much (*turns to Nike*). Nike, remember the daughter of whom you are. We have brought you up all these years as a decent Christian. It is now up to you to show the world what stuff you are made of. We have brought you here to study, do not disgrace us. Do not disappoint us. We shall be going now. We leave you in God's able hands. He will take good care of you.

MOTHER: Do not forget to warm your stew otherwise it will spoil. When you go to the market, price the things very well because these city people are always looking for who to cheat.

NIKE: I will ma.

FATHER: Take this money. Manage it very well my dear. You know payday is still very far. We will send more money and foodstuff through our pastor in two weeks. He will be coming to the city for a synod meeting.

NIKE: (*kneels down*). Thank you very much father. Please greet my brothers and sisters. I am missing them already (*Nike starts sobbing. Her mother also follows suit*).

FATHER: (*touched, but putting on a brave show*). Hm, these women have started again. My wife, Oya[7], let us go home, abi[8] you too want to read medicine? All right my daughters, goodbye. Take good care of yourselves (*father and mother leave. Nike continues to sob*).

LANRE: (*goes to Nike*). Why are you behaving like a baby, did you think you would live with your parents forever? You better cheer up. Universities are for grown ups, not babies. Have you ever seen a baby doctor?

DEOLA: (*sarcastically*). Leave her alone. Na bobo and shakara[9] combined! That is how they all react when they first arrive at the university. I give her two weeks of October rush[10] and she will be a transformed girl.

LANRE: Do you think it is good for us to go out tonight and leave her alone?

DEOLA: (*shocked*). Why not? What's wrong with you? Have you suddenly become a babysitter?

LANRE: I think it is the milk of human kindness welling up in me. Anyway, maybe Dupe will come in before we go. They can stay together and talk medicine.

DEOLA: Are you kidding? As if you don't know Dupe. That one is married to her medical books. She won't come back until very late, I am sure (*pause*). Well, if you are so worried about leaving her behind, why don't we take her with us?

LANRE: To the party?

DEOLA: Where else?

LANRE: (*scandalized*). Her father said we should look after her. He did not say we should corrupt her!

DEOLA: (*laughs*). Corruption indeed. You know we may be doing her a good turn by introducing her to the other side of life. The girl cannot remain ignorant for the rest of her life. Besides, these parties cannot have too many girls. They are always in demand.

LANRE: Well, I do hope you know what you are doing (*she turns to Nike*). Are you feeling better now?

NIKE: (*still heaving with suppressed sobs*). Yes, thank you very much. I am feeling much better.

DEOLA: We are going out tonight, will you like to go with us?

NIKE: Going out? I suppose you know a lot of places. Where are you going?

DEOLA: We are going to a party. Do you like parties?

NIKE: Parties? I have never been to a night party before. All the birthday parties in the village take place in the afternoon.

DEOLA: Those are children's parties. We are talking about adults' parties.

NIKE: Adults' parties? I have never been to one before.

LANRE: There's always a first time to everything. Maybe you will start today.

NIKE: (*gets up from the bed*). This is my party dress and it is rather dusty from the trip. You know the road from our village is not tarred.

DEOLA: (*shocked*). This?

LANRE: No kidding?

NIKE: Yes, this is what I used to wear to the birthday parties at home (*proudly*). My mother made it for me when I was in form four.

DEOLA: (*sarcastically*). Indeed, it shows. Let's look through your luggage and see whether there is something more appropriate for adults' parties (*she starts going through Nike's bag and flings each successive gown away in disgust. Finally she looks up in dismay and draws Lanre aside*).

LANRE: What is the verdict?

DEOLA: The verdict is: if you want her to tag along, you lend or give her a dress.

LANRE: Why me? You are the one who went to America to shop.

DEOLA: No dice. All the clothes in that wardrobe, I sweated before I got them.

LANRE: Why don't we even ask her whether she has money to buy a new dress?

DEOLA: Okay (*goes back to Nike*). Nike, all these things you brought with you will not do at all. Most of them are out of fashion. Some are even faded. Why don't we go to the shops now and buy you something from your pocket money? You are no longer a village girl. You must dress like a university undergraduate now, a medical student for that matter.

NIKE: The money my father gave to me is supposed to last me till the end of the month. I don't know whether I will be able to buy a dress from it.

LANRE: Pardon my curiosity, but how much is it?

NIKE: Five Hundred Naira.

LANRE: Five Hundred what?

DEOLA: Five Hundred Naira?

NIKE: Is it too much?

DEOLA: Too much my foot! That kind of money cannot last you for a day here. It can't even buy you earrings for the party.

LANRE: What shall we do?

DEOLA: (*stands up and speaks in an aside*). Well, I think she should wear the same size as I do. But my feet are bigger than hers, more like your size. So, I'll give her a dress, and you give her a pair of shoes. We can then look through our jewelry boxes and give her whatever pieces of costume jewelries that we can spare.

LANRE: Give or lend?

DEOLA: Don't be mean. I am not saying you should give her the bottom of your box. After all, you are the one playing mother hen (*she turns to Nike*). Nike we have decided to give you the things you need for the party.

NIKE: Thank you very much. You are so kind. How can I ever thank you enough?

DEOLA: Don't worry; you too will do the same thing for a Jambite one day.

LANRE: We have to hurry up. You know we haven't fixed our hair.

DEOLA: Oh that's right. We have to go to the salon. Nike, you will have to loosen your hair when we are going to the party. Nobody ties her hair with thread like that anymore.

NIKE: My hair too? But this is the latest style in the village. It is called 'sun gas'[11] (*both Deola and Lanre laugh*).

Lights Fade Out

Scene 2

Set, same as before. Nike is asleep on her bed. She is the only one in the room. Door opens and Dupe comes in with lab coat over her arm.

DUPE: Oh yeah, our Jambite has come!

NIKE: (*wakes up*). Oh, I thought it was Deola and Lanre.

DUPE: No, I am Dupe. I am sorry I woke you. So you've already met my roommates. Good. I am Dupe Ajenifuja. I am in Part three Medicine. What is your name?

NIKE: I am Nike Adedara. I have just been admitted to read Medicine through Direct Entry.

DUPE: Medicine? Great! I am pleased to meet you. I hope you will enjoy your stay in this room and in the University as well. If you have any academic problem, I'll be very willing to help.

NIKE: Thank you very much. Is it true that Medicine is very tough?

DUPE: To lazy people, everything is tough, but if you are hard working, you will see it as a challenge.

NIKE: I do believe I am hard working. I had 'A's in all my GCE A Level papers and I took the exams at home.

DUPE: Great! That is the stuff of people who can withstand the college of Medicine here. How are you settling down? What are you doing tonight? There is a lecture titled "Abortion and its side effects", which is going to be delivered by Professor Hamstrung. I think it will be a very good opportunity for you to be introduced to the medical circle.

NIKE: Oh, I am afraid I can't go. Deola and Lanre have been kind enough to invite me to a party and I have already given my word that I'll go with them.

DUPE: (*disappointed*). Hmm, so you have already chosen the fast lane. A word of caution though, always remember what you are here for. You have a bright future ahead of you. Don't mess up your life for some transient enjoyment (*shakes her head*). Have you bought your books?

NIKE: Books? No, I haven't. I don't have the list of books yet.

DUPE: I will advise you to buy the books early so that you can get down to serious reading as soon as possible. The books are quite expensive. I hope you know that?

NIKE: My father gave me five hundred Naira. I hope it will be all right?

DUPE: Five hundred what? The cheapest book you can hope to buy is a Pocket Medical Dictionary and it will cost at least One Thousand Naira.

NIKE: My God! How am I going to be able to afford them? My father is just a poor headmaster. We are not rich at all.

DUPE: That brings me back to the issue of seriousness. If you are hardworking, you can win a scholarship. I am from a humble background too. It is because I won a scholarship that things are a bit easy for me. A university is not for partying alone. You have to be serious with your academics (*gets up*). If I don't want to be late for that lecture, I have to get ready now (*heads for bathroom*).

NIKE: My God, what am I going to do? My parents cannot afford a very expensive education for me. I have three sisters and four brothers, all still in the primary and secondary schools.

DUPE: (*comes in from the bathroom*). Are you sure you don't want to change your mind and come along?

NIKE: Oh, not tonight (*Deola and Lanre enter*).

DEOLA: Ah, the only living female Doc-in-training! How you dey[12]? You mean you actually found time to prise yourself away from your books early enough to come to the room before twelve midnight?

DUPE: Deola you bugger! How you dey yourself? What's happening tonight?

DEOLA: We lesser mortals are going to a party.

DUPE: As usual. This fresh medic tells me she is going with you.

DEOLA: Yes, she is.

DUPE: Well, all I have to say is 'don't let the fast lane turn her head'.

LANRE: Doc, Doc! You think everybody will be like you? All work and no play …

DEOLA: Makes Jill a dull girl!

DUPE: Girls, I am not saying you should not have fun, but then, keep an eye on the GPA[13]. I'll be seeing you (goes out).

B: (*turns to Nike who appears lost in thought*) Nike, why do you look so down in the mouth? Has Dupe been painting us black to you?

NIKE: (*as if she is alone*). This education is certainly an expensive one. Maybe I should defer my admission for a session, go and get a job so that I can save some money. That seems to be my only hope of becoming a doctor (*Deola stops her in her tracks*).

DEOLA: That is one option.

NIKE: (*looking up expectantly*). You have another option?

DEOLA: (*moves to sit beside her*). Let me ask you a question. Do you have a boyfriend?

NIKE: (*bashful*). Well, Mr. Jackson, a teacher in my former school was pestering me to become his girlfriend.

DEOLA: And what is Mr. Jackson's qualification if I may ask?

NIKE: He is an NCE[14] holder.

DEOLA: When did he qualify?

NIKE: Two years ago.

DEOLA: Which means he will be on a salary of Fifteen Thousand Naira per month. If ever you intend to succumb to his 'pestering', his whole salary for two months cannot buy your medical books for a semester, not to talk of clothes, shoes, etc.

NIKE: That is why I want to go and work.

DEOLA: There is another option. When you put your yam in the fire, you then start looking round for the knife. In plain language, you can have your boyfriend who is a security...

NIKE: Security?

DEOLA: I mean somebody you will eventually marry. He may be a poor and young person like your Jackson, but at the same time, you have some 'securities' that foot all the bills. They provide the financial base that is necessary for all modern girls. Through their largesse, some smart girls travel abroad regularly and even buy cars on their tickets.

NIKE: Eh? Is that what is called scholarships?

LANRE: Scholarships indeed! They are called sugar daddies.

NIKE: Sugar daddies? What do I have to give them to make them so generous?

LANRE: Nothing much. You care for them; you comfort them and make them happy.

NIKE: Simple as that?

DEOLA: Why is this girl so dumb? You go to bed with them.

NIKE: (*scandalized*). Go to bed with them? How many of them?

LANRE: As many as you are lucky to land of course.

NIKE: But I am a virgin.

DEOLA: A what?

LANRE: Virgin?

DEOLA: Are you crazy? How old are you?

NIKE: I am eighteen years old

DEOLA: I hope there is nothing psychologically wrong with you? How can you be eighteen and still be a virgin? Are all the boys in your village blind or they are too ugly for your liking?

NIKE: Well, we have been told not to go into sex before marriage.

LANRE: Nonsense. What if you end up marrying somebody who is impotent or that has a strange disease?

DEOLA: That is even a minor thing. If you want to survive in this system, you have to get rid of this your ridiculous virginity. Your body is your asset. You have to use it wisely to enable it make money for you.

NIKE: I don't know about that. I want to get married as a virgin.

DEOLA: (*gets up in* annoyance). That's right. It is your decision. Whoever is going for this party should start dressing up.

LANRE: (*hugging herself and with a dreamy expression on her face*). Sure, I'm all set to have a nice time.

Blackout

Scene 3

Set, the same as in the previous scene. The girls are all in the room. Deola, Lanre and Nike are asleep on their beds. Dupe is bustling about, singing and getting ready for school.

DEOLA: (*emerging from under her bedclothes*). Damnit, Dupe, what is wrong with you, can't you allow innocent people to sleep in peace?

DUPE: I'm sorry, Deola, but it is 8:00 a.m. already and today is Friday, a school day. Aren't you going to school?

LANRE: (*joining the conversation*). Sharrap girl, everyday no be Christmas now, even lecturers dey take day-off[15].

DUPE: So you have become a lecturer now? Anyway, have a nice day. I am off to school (*moves to Nike's bed and taps her awake*). New Medico, I hope you will come to the Faculty for your registration today.

NIKE: (*lifting up her head*). Oh, is it morning already? Ha, when will the registration start?

DUPE: Ten o'clock.

NIKE: I will be there.

DUPE: See you later then (*she exits*).

The other three girls get up from their beds.

LANRE: Boy! That was some party!

DEOLA: Are you telling me? It is better to attend parties thrown by these senior boys than all the young boys' disco parties.

NIKE: I have never seen that kind of thing before. Look at the dresses worn by some of the women. Some were just glittering like glass. Some shoes were so beautiful that I felt if I were to be the owner I would not be able to walk on the dirty ground with them.

LANRE: You have not seen anything at all. This was just a small naming ceremony party. If it were to be a more serious one, you would just faint from astonishment.

NIKE: When I saw the interior of that house, I almost fainted. Wall to wall rug, mirrors everywhere, beautiful pictures, my God, some people have money.

LANRE: Eh! But the party took place outside the house, how did you get inside?

NIKE: (*she is embarrassed as Deola and Lanre laugh uproariously*). I admired the front view and Chief Ewuoso offered to take me inside.

DEOLA: (*sarcastically*). And of course you went like a lamb to the slaughter! I am sure that annoying virginity has now been taken care of.

NIKE: Of course not. Do you think I will allow any man to take me to bed just like that?

DEOLA: (*getting down from the bed*). We shall see. Time will tell, but for now. It is time to get ready for school, girls. Lanre, we have missed our eight o'clock class, we shouldn't miss the one at ten o'clock.

LANRE: That is very true. One word of warning to you though, Nike, I saw the way Chief Agbabiaka was eyeing you last night. He belongs to me. Don't trespass.

NIKE: Chief Agbabiaka? I can't even remember who that is (*Lanre goes to the bathroom. Nike faces Deola*). By the way, how much money were you sprayed[16] with last night? I counted my own and it was five hundred and fifty Naira.

DEOLA: Who cares about chicken stuff like that? I use the money to spray other dancers immediately I receive it. There is another serious party tomorrow night. When we come back from lectures today, I will take you to the shopping center so that we can buy you a respectable Iro and Buba,[17] complete with head tie. You can't be wearing the same thing to all the parties.

NIKE: Ah, but I want to spend this money on books.

DEOLA: Books will come later. Don't worry. Let us first of all deck you out in some respectable attire and see how much more your admirers will spray you. It is an investment.

NIKE: Okay, if you say so.

Blackout

Scene 4

Set, same as in the last scene. It is the night after the party. Deola is asleep on her bed. Lanre is sitting up on her bed and glowering at nobody in particular. Dupe is busy dressing for Church, adjusting her hat in front of the mirror.

DUPE: Lanre, what's wrong with you? Your face tells me you are thinking unholy thoughts, quite unfit for a Sunday morning. Who are you planning to beat up?

LANRE: (*in anger*). Ah, she could have fooled me. All the pretence about being innocent and all. It was a big hoax. If I can just lay my hands upon her now, she will not forget me in a hurry.

DUPE: Who?

LANRE: Your false medic of course.

DUPE: You mean Nike? What happened to her?

LANRE: The stupid girl. We went to a party yesterday and she went home with my boyfriend.

DEOLA: (*emerging from beneath her bed clothes, laughs*). Boyfriend or man-friend ? I don't know what you are moaning about. You have to look at these things with a professional eye. The winner takes it all. Nobody wins all the time my girl. Please follow Dupe to Church and let me sleep in peace (*goes back under bedclothes*).

DUPE: (*annoyed*). So you have spoilt this girl's life. I knew it; I knew it would happen this way. I hope she will not be too hurt before she turns back.

LANRE: I hope she rots in hell.

Blackout

Scene 5

Set, same as before. Dupe is reading by her bed. Nike comes in smartly dressed, complete with new hair-do and make-up.

DUPE: Hmm, quite a different girl from the one I saw two months ago.

NIKE: (*laughs*). A lot of water has passed under the bridge. How's life with you?

DUPE: Fine, thank God. What's been happening to you? You have not come to this room since you went for that party almost two months ago.

NIKE: (*laughs*). Oh, that party. Well, I went for the party and I met this man (*laughs in an embarrassed manner*). He's a young ... well, let's say middle-aged man. He fell in love with me and I fell in love with him. So, there you are. I live in his house now.

DUPE: Are you married to him?

NIKE: Well ... no.

DUPE: Why don't you marry him and stop living in sin.

NIKE: Ah … um … There is a short hitch there you see. He got married to a woman about ten years ago. He later discovered that the woman was being unfaithful to him, so he drove her out of the house. He however didn't bother to obtain a divorce because he felt all women were alike and he didn't want to marry again. Then he met me. He couldn't believe that a girl as old as me could be a virgin. He was completely knocked over. So, he will start divorce proceedings against that woman soon so that we can be married.

DUPE: Do you actually believe this man?

NIKE: Absolutely! He loves me so much; he cannot bear to live without me. Actually he didn't want me to come and sleep in the hostel, but I told him that my parents would be visiting me today.

DUPE: Oh, so your parents are coming. That is why you have come here today. Interesting! (*changing the subject*). How are you finding your lectures? I hope you have been able to buy your books?

NIKE: I am actually enjoying the lectures. I have bought all the recommended textbooks. The Monday after the party, Chief took me out shopping. He bought me a new wardrobe- clothes, shoes, jewelries, name it, he bought everything for me. He took me to a salon, I did my hair, my finger and toenails and I bought a makeup kit. Then he took me to a bookshop and bought all my books for me. The man really loves me and I love him too.

DUPE: (quietly). Are you sure it's him you love or his money?

NIKE: (*flustered*). Dupe, you are incorrigible (*gets up*). I want to change into my 'old faithfuls' before my parents come. This new 'transformed me' will be too much for them (*she changes and cleans off her makeup*). I hope Lanre is not around. I do not want any ugly scene especially when my parents are around. You know Chief used to go out with her.

DUPE: But can't you see even from that small incident that the man can be very unscrupulous?

NIKE: (*exasperated*). Dupe, can we change the subject please? (*a knock on the door*).

DUPE: Come in?

NIKE: Yes? (*Nike's parents enter. She rushes towards them and embraces them*). Papa, Mama, oh, I'm so glad to see you.

FATHER: How are you my daughter?

DUPE: You are welcome sir.

MOTHER: How are you young lady?

DUPE: I am fine ma.

NIKE: What of my brothers and sisters? You should have brought one or two of them.

FATHER: We wanted to bring them. They all cried and cried, but we did not have the transport fare to bring them. Actually, they have not paid our salary for last month. We were only able to come today because some of your mother's customers paid her some long outstanding debts.

NIKE: You shouldn't have bothered. I still have some money left over from what you sent through the pastor.

MOTHER: Ah, my good daughter, I knew you would not spend carelessly. We brought you some foodstuff for cooking.

NIKE: (*looks through the parcel*). Actually, Mother, I do not cook anymore. It is better to eat at the cafeteria. You see, I need the time to read my books.

FATHER: It is true my daughter. That means your money ought to have finished by now. I was able to borrow some money so that you will be able to buy some books and other necessities. This is Two Thousand Naira. You can use the change for your feeding for the rest of the month.

NIKE: Thank you Papa.

FATHER: (*surprised*). Nike (*holds her hand*). What has happened to your fingernails within two months? Look at your hair too; I hope you have not joined any bad gang here?

NIKE: (*defensive*). Papa you mean you don't trust me? You should know that village ways are different from city ways. I cannot leave my fingernails and hair like they were before. Do you want me to feel inferior to my mates?

FATHER: My daughter, I brought you up to have a mind of your own, to know what is good and what is bad, to know what you want and what you do not want, to know what is good for you and what is not good for you. Are you now telling me that you have found it better to blend with the crowd?

NIKE: Papa, no, I'm still the same daughter you reared. Don't worry. I have not changed.

MOTHER: (*doubtfully*). I hope everything is all right.

NIKE: Em, please next time … eh … when you want to give me money, just buy postal order and post it to me.

FATHER: (*confused*). You mean we should not bring the money here again?

MOTHER: (rummages in her bag). That reminds me, Mr. Jackson sent this letter to you.

NIKE: Why is he writing me now? (*takes the letter and drops it on her bed*).

FATHER: As if you don't know! Do you want us to take a reply? Not that it would help anyway, he has left our village and he might not have time to visit us for a long time to come.

NIKE: He has left? That is good for him. I think you should leave now. I have some assignments to submit tomorrow.

FATHER: (*beaming with pride*). Ah, my own doctor, my very own doctor, I hope you can now diagnose and cure ailments?

MOTHER: Nike, your grandmother has been feeling quite sickly lately. Bring your equipment when you are coming home for the holidays so that you will be able to give her an injection.

NIKE: Mama, it is not doctors that give injections, it is the nurses.

MOTHER: Ah, you better learn that one too. That one will really impress the people in the village.

FATHER: All right. Let us go. So we are not allowed to come and visit you again? I so much wanted to go round the campus. I thought you would be able to show us round the place today. I will have to wait for your graduation day, or maybe during the holidays.

NIKE: (*impatiently*). Yes Papa, during the holidays will be fine. You simply have to go now.

MOTHER: What of Deola and Lanre, should we not leave some cocoyams for them?

NIKE: No, they do not cook either. I'll tell them you asked after them (*she ushers them out*).

MOTHER: (*to Dupe*). Goodbye my daughter.

FATHER: (*to Dupe*). Goodbye. Greet your roommates.

DUPE: Thank you, goodbye (*Nike exits with her parents*). What a shame (*Nike returns*). Nike, that performance was quite unkind of you. Are you now so ashamed of your parents that you cannot bear them to visit you? You cannot even take them round the campus and make them feel proud of you.

NIKE: I'm so ashamed of myself. I feel quite sick at my behavior towards them. You see, I love them so much and I do not want them to encounter Lanre's fury. She has been threatening all around that she would have a showdown with me. I am not afraid of her, but I do not want her to hurt or disillusion my parents. I feel very bad.

DUPE: (*after a long pause*). Aren't you going to read your letter?

NIKE: (*moves towards it and picks it up*). My letter! My letter. Do I really want to read it? Do I really want to know what it contains? I used to be very fond of the guy that wrote it. I used to dream of the day when I would give myself to him. I have nothing to give to him again. No more innocence to bestow upon Jackson.

DUPE: At least, you should read what he has to say to you.

NIKE: I might as well read and destroy it. Chief must not see it (*reads*).
My darling Nike,
I hope this letter meets you in good health. How are you settling down in your new environment? I trust that the work there is not overwhelming. I really do miss you, but I believe it is just for a brief period of time that we shall be separated. I miss the sunshine of your smile, which dispels the cloudiest sky. I miss your voice that tinkles like a bell and brings joy to many souls. I miss you because you are kind. I miss you because you are caring. I look forward to the day when we shall be reunited (*she sighs*). I have good news for you. I have been offered admission into the University to study Law. Now, more than ever, I regret not choosing the same university that you did. I hope to visit you soon and we'll really talk. I wish you all the best in your studies.
Yours,
Jackson.
(*she sighs*)

DUPE: It wasn't all that difficult to read, was it?

NIKE: (*as if in a reverie*). Chief does not treat me like this. He doesn't waste sweet words on me. Most of the time, he is away, tending his business. "The business that has provided your nest for you" he says, anytime I complain. (*Smiles*) But what would it be like to be married to Jackson? To be married to a man of my age, of the same academic and intellectual quality as myself. We would then be able to rub minds together even as we rub our bodies together. With Chief, the rubbing is only on one level, and that is the physical.

DUPE: If there is so much disparity why don't you break away from Chief?

NIKE: (*shrugging her shoulders as if in defeat*). I have made my bed; I have to lie on it. I'm holding on to Chief because he can provide me with the education that I want without having to sweat too much for it. I love Jackson's kind of life, but it is too late to have it. I am no longer innocent. Which other man would want me again after I have been another man's mistress?

DUPE: I think you are trying to measure every man by Chief's standard. There are still many men who are able to love because of other qualities apart from beauty and your so-called innocence. You are being unfair to Jackson. Why don't you give him a chance?

NIKE: (*throws up her hands in exasperation and starts changing her dress again*). I don't want to think about it. I don't think I'll sleep here after all. I don't want to encounter Lanre. I am going back to my nest (*tries to sound breezy*). I'll see you some other time. Thanks for trying to talk me out of my new lifestyle, but the nest beckons (*she turns to go*).

DUPE: Nike, are you sure it is a nest or a cage?

NIKE: (*pauses*). Yes, I think it is a nest (*becoming confused*) ... that is ... it was a nest, and then it became a cage. I think it is a nest in a cage ... yes, a nest in a cage.

DUPE: Why don't you break out now that you still have a chance?

NIKE: (*slowly*). No, my dear sister, it is too late (*moves as if to go*).

DUPE: Too late? Why do you say it is too late?

NIKE: (*stops in her tracks, still facing the door and pauses*). Dupe, I am pregnant.

DUPE: (*shocked. Gets up and goes to her*). No.

NIKE: Yes, I am pregnant.

DUPE: (*quietly*). You had better make sure he gets that divorce then.

NIKE: He will. That is not the problem.

DUPE: What seems to be the problem then?

NIKE: He wants me to abort the pregnancy.

DUPE: Abort? I hope you do not intend to do that?

NIKE: (*turns to Dupe defensively*). Why not? He says if his wife gets to know that somebody is pregnant for him, she might turn the table against him and become the accuser instead of the accused.

DUPE: What's so bad in that? He deserves to be accused.

NIKE: Well, he wants me to have an abortion. It will also disturb my academics if I keep the pregnancy.

DUPE: Do you know that boys in this University have various names for girls here?

NIKE: What type of names?

DUPE: Oh, there are many of them. I will just mention two examples that are relevant to our discussion here. They sometimes categorize girls into two - motherless babies and babyless mothers.

NIKE: What do they mean by the names?

DUPE: Motherless babies are the young girls like you who come into the University, still needing their mothers' guidance and direction. Because the mothers are not around, such girls misbehave.

NIKE: What of babyless mothers?

DUPE: Babyless mothers are the girls that have led wayward lives and aborted pregnancies many times. As a result of the pregnancies, they can be categorized as mothers, but they have no baby to show for the experience.

NIKE: (*disgusted*). That is very morbid.

DUPE: You are toying with your whole life when you toy with the issue of abortion like that.

NIKE: (*defiantly*). There is no big deal about abortion. People do it everyday and get away with it. I know Deola and Lanre have had series of abortions and it does not show on them.

DUPE: it does not show on them? That is what you think. Have you ever wondered why both of them are so promiscuous today? Is it not because of that first abortion that they "got away with" to use your expression?

NIKE: Well, maybe.

DUPE: Maybe? I tell you with certainty that they became more promiscuous because they felt, and still feel, that all it costs is a D & C; but with each abortion they commit, they become more and more emotionally hardened. They are becoming hardened criminals, so to speak, committing murder upon murder.

NIKE: But the fetus is not yet a human being.

DUPE: That fetus inside you is a part of you. It is attached to you, feeding on you, trusting you to take care of it. Have you ever seen a baby with its small chubby arms clasped tightly round its mother's neck at the approach of a stranger?

NIKE: Many times.

DUPE: That is how that fetus is clinging to you trustingly, expecting love and protection from you. Then you take your baby to a doctor, who yanks him or her out by brute force from your womb.

NIKE: (*shaken*). You are just being emotional and moralistic about this matter.

DUPE: Am I? I have heard testimonies of women who suffered post abortion syndrome. They experienced recurrent recollections and dreams about their babies being destroyed. This usually results in lack of interest in life, low self esteem, depression and a host of other psychological and emotional problems. Do you want that to be your experience in life?

NIKE: No.

DUPE: From the little I've seen of you, you have a childlike and bubbly disposition. You are not a mercenary at heart. Such an act of murder will definitely affect you psychologically.

NIKE: (*defensively*). I have grown up since you first met me.

DUPE: Nevertheless, many women, well versed in the ways of the world, still suffer from these things. I have come across many cases as a medical student. For example, some barren women who had committed abortions in the past find it impossible to forgive themselves. A popular American actress, Shelley Winters, broke down in tears during a discussion programme on television and said "I've committed two abortions in my life, and now, I'm a very lonely woman.

I would give up everything – my money, my academy awards, my career – if only I could have those children now".

NIKE: You mean she broke down right there on television with millions of viewers watching her?

DUPE: Yes, she did. That shows how depressed and guilty she felt. That was a woman of the world. You are just a young, innocent and misguided girl. Let me give you another example. The great American star, Gloria Swanson, began and ended her autobiography with lamentations over her aborted child. She aborted the pregnancy to preserve her reputation. Fifty four years later, in 1979, when she turned eighty-four, she said- oh let us read it together from her book (*she gets up, searches through her shelf and brings out the book. She reads*). "The greatest regret of my life has always been that I didn't have my baby, Henri's child, in 1925. Nothing in the whole world is worth a baby. I realized as soon as it was too late, and I never stopped blaming myself"(*she closes the book*). So, Nike, you have read this yourself. Do you want to be lamenting at eighty-four too?

NIKE: I do not know anymore. I have to go now (*moves to go*).

DUPE: By the way, you did not even ask after Deola.

NIKE: I do not want to see her.

DUPE: That is a pity because she deserves all the sympathy she can get now.

NIKE: Why?

DUPE: She is in hospital now.

NIKE: Hospital? What is wrong with her?

DUPE: She has had one abortion too many.

NIKE: What?

DUPE: Yes, she went to a private clinic where she normally goes for her D & C and the doctor perforated her womb so badly. She was rushed to the teaching hospital and the whole womb had to be removed.

NIKE: Ah, so she cannot have children anymore?

DUPE: No. She can never have children in her life. Right now, the main concern is how she would survive. She is in a very bad shape.

NIKE: I can't take anymore (*she storms out of the room*).

DUPE: I have a very strong sense of foreboding that this girl will strongly regret not taking my advice today (*she resumes her reading. Lanre enters as if in a hurry*).

LANRE: Hi Dupe. Have you seen Nike?

DUPE: Yes, she just left here about thirty minutes ago.

LANRE: Oh, I missed her. What a shame! I wanted to come and have a showdown with her. Did her parents come?

DUPE: Yes they did.

LANRE: Oh what a lost opportunity. I wanted to come and tell them what their daughter has become.

DUPE: (*storms up in annoyance*). And would your conscience have allowed you to do such a thing? Who introduced her to this kind of life, was it not you? You, and that Deola of a girl. She is reaping the fruits of her labor, groaning on the hospital bed now. You! Do you think you will get away with everything? You will be surprised. You will definitely reap what you have sown.

LANRE: (*shocked*). Well, well, well! I have never seen this side of you before. Why are you so angry? Whatever you may say though, I will still write a letter to her parents giving them her new address. I know Chief very well, before this first semester is over, he will throw her over. He is always in love till the next pretty face shows up. It will be real fun having her back in this room with us lesser mortals, and with a broken heart too.

DUPE: Don't tell me you suffered from heartbreak when he threw you over (*gets up in anger*). I think I need some fresh air. You have quite polluted the air here (*she picks her jacket and a letter falls out of her pocket*). There, that is for you. I wonder why I picked it for you. I know it will be from one of your fornicating partners (*she exits in annoyance*).

LANRE: (*laughs*). Thanks all the same. Even if I have not been able to catch Nike today, at least I have succeeded in upsetting Dupe. So Deola is in Hospital? I wondered where she was going when she packed her bag and refused to tell me. Must be another D & C case (*begins to open letter*). Oh, this letter must be from my boyfriend, Tola. It is postmarked Kaduna. This should at least cheer me up (*sits down and begins to read*).

Lanre dear,

It has been good while it lasted. You girls always think we guys don't know (*wrinkles her face in puzzlement*). But you'll be surprised to hear that I know about your sugar daddies, both while I was on campus and since I've been here. I know you have been trying to use me as a 'security', but I'm sorry, I'm not a fool. I hereby enclose my wedding invitation in this letter. I'll be getting married next week Saturday- the last day of November. Judging by the postal services in our dear country, you will receive this letter about a week after the occasion. Wish us well. I wish you happy hunting after the sugar daddies. They are sweet, aren't they, especially the cash?

Bye,

Tola

(*She rushes to calendar*). What is today's date? Oh no, December 5. It is done (*becoming hysterical*). No, I can't believe this. This cannot be true. It is just a bad dream. Please, can somebody wake me up and tell me it was a dream? (*she sobs hysterically*).

Blackout

PART TWO

Scene 1

Chief Agbabiaka's residence. A very plush sitting room. Nike is moving about, enjoying the splendor. She is holding a cocktail glass from which she sips. The bell rings and she goes to open the door. She is shocked at what she sees. She slams the door and runs back inside. The door opens from outside and her parents enter.

NIKE: Papa, Mama, what are you doing here?

FATHER: That is the question we should be asking you. What are you doing here? Is this where your mother and I put you? Is this where you are studying your medicine? Answer me fast before I daze your face with ten slaps.

MOTHER: Adenike, what has brought you to this situation? You did not think of the disgrace you have brought upon your family. If not for your roommate, Lanre who wrote us, we wouldn't have known anything about the matter.

NIKE: Oh, so she wrote, I should have known.

FATHER: Known what, I say known what? So you have now become a prostitute in the city. Oh, the gods of my fathers, are you sleeping in the sky that my daughter has now become a public slut?

NIKE: Father, I am not a prostitute. I am in my boyfriend's house. Did Lanre tell you that I have more than one boyfriend?

FATHER: Boyfriend? Boyfriend? You call a married man a boyfriend? Do you think I will be alive and see you becoming a second wife? Look, look at his picture on the wall, this man should be the same age with me and she calls him boyfriend.

MOTHER: It is not right my daughter, do not spoil another woman's home. Allow God to build your own home for you.

NIKE: The marriage had already broken before I came onto the scene at all. They are planning to get officially divorced now. That is what we are waiting for to enable us get married.

FATHER: And you couldn't wait it out in your room on the campus? You had to move in with him like a girl that does not have any moral whatsoever. If he throws you out one day, do you think any self-respecting man would take you up?

NIKE: It will not happen like that. He loves me so much. You see, he bought all my books for me. He bought clothes for me …

FATHER: (*sadly*). You are a big disappointment. You mean you could allow another man to take over your father's responsibility? While I am still alive, you gave my responsibilities to another man to perform? Now, pack your things and let us go.

NIKE: No Papa. I know your abilities. The Two Thousand Naira you gave me the other day could only have bought one textbook. I know you couldn't afford to give me more. I can't just leave this place like this.

FATHER: For the last time Nike, pack your things and let us go.

NIKE: (*begging on her knees, sobbing*). Please Papa, don't make me leave like this.

FATHER: (*shoulders slumped in defeat*). I had always thought I had my daughter's confidence. So you couldn't call me, sit me down and let us talk it over together? Even if I had to go and obtain a loan or something, we could have managed somehow. You have rejected me as your father. I am now rejecting you as my child. It breaks my heart, but thank God, a big head cannot go completely bald. There will still remain patches of hair on some parts of the scalp. I still have my other children. They will not fail me. My wife let us go. Nike, Let me never see your face again (*he shakes his head and exits*).

MOTHER: My daughter Nike, is this how you have turned my face towards the setting sun? Ah, the very first child of my youth, the very first fruit of my womb, is this how you disgrace and reject us? (*she looks longingly at Nike, then turns and moves towards the door. She looks back as if to say something, changes her mind and slowly exits*).

NIKE: (*sobbing intensifies as they exit*). Is it worth it? Is it really worth it staying in this cage? I lost my innocence in it; I have lost my parents too in it. Is it worth it, is it really worth it? (*she continues sobbing and Chief enters*).

CHIEF: Aa ah Nike, what is the matter with you?

NIKE: Oh Chief, my life has turned upside down. Lanre wrote to my parents and they came here today. They wanted me to leave with them but I couldn't just leave you like that. So, my father said he has rejected me as his child (*fresh sobbing*).

CHIEF: (*offhandedly*). Is that why you are crying like that? You should have followed them. We would have settled everything later.

NIKE: (*shocked*). Chief, what do you mean?

CHIEF: It is not all that important. Anyway, wipe your face and let us talk. I've brought my doctor to come and have a talk with you about this abortion business.

NIKE: Really?

CHIEF: Yes. You are being unnecessarily old-fashioned about the issue. I tell you, it is very safe. Shall I ask him to come in?

NIKE: (*pulling herself together with difficulty. She gets up and paces up and down aimlessly*). Yes, bring him in (*Chief goes out*). It never rains, it pours. I am beginning to see the meanness and selfishness in this man. If he thinks I am going to wreck my life through an abortion, he is mistaken.

CHIEF: (*enters with an elderly man*). Nike, this is Dr. Dagunduro. Doctor, this is Nike.

NIKE: Pleased to meet you Doctor (*extends hand to Doctor*).

DOCTOR: (*shaking Nike's hand*). The pleasure is mine madam.

NIKE: Please be seated.

CHIEF: (*draws Nike aside*). Dr. Dagunduro has been my doctor for years. He will educate you on the matter we have been talking about. After that, he will take you to his private clinic and do what is necessary. Then we will be able to plan for the trip to America to shop for our wedding during your semester break.

NIKE: (*without enthusiasm*) I see!

CHIEF: (breezily). Well, I will leave you two to it. I have to get back to the office. I have a lot of work to do. Nike, be a good girl and cooperate with Doctor Dagunduro. Doctor, I'll see you later (*he goes*).

NIKE: Doctor, can I offer you a drink before we start the discussion?

DOCTOR: Yes madam, whisky on the rocks if you have it.

NIKE: (*with heavy sarcasm*). Oh Doctor, we have everything in this cushy nest, except the things that really matter (*she goes to the in-built bar and prepares Doctor's drink. As she brings it over, Doctor looks at her with an expression of puzzlement*).

DOCTOR: Thank you very much madam (*he leaves the drink untouched*).

NIKE: (*takes a sip from her drink*). Why don't you drink up and let's start the discussion.

DOCTOR: (*sighs*). You know, you remind me of somebody?

NIKE: Really? Who is that?

DOCTOR: My youngest daughter.

NIKE: Is that so? I will really like to meet her, at least so that I can know what I look like.

DOCTOR: I'm afraid it won't be possible.

NIKE: Why not? Does she live abroad?

DOCTOR: If she lived abroad she could be reached, but I'm afraid she now lives in heaven or hell, I don't know for sure where she ended up.

NIKE: She's dead?

DOCTOR: Yes. She died, just last year.

NIKE: Oh, I'm sorry. What killed her?

DOCTOR: She had a ruptured ectopic pregnancy.

NIKE: What is ectopic pregnancy?

DOCTOR: it is a pregnancy that develops in the fallopian tube instead of descending into the womb. When the pregnancy starts developing, the tube bursts and it sometimes proves to be fatal.

NIKE: What a pity! But why does the pregnancy stay in the tube instead of moving into the womb?

DOCTOR: it happens when the tube is blocked.

NIKE: What blocks the tubes?

DOCTOR: There can be many reasons. It could be because of an infection that was not treated, through sexually transmitted diseases, and of course … (*pauses*) but that does not matter.

NIKE: Doctor, I have a feeling that it matters. What were you going to say?

DOCTOR: (*embarrassed. He gets up and starts pacing the room*). Em … er … well, I was going to say a blocked tube could also result from infection contacted during an abortion procedure. This may eventually lead to ectopic pregnancy or infertility.

NIKE: (*gets up and kneels in front of the doctor and holds his hands*). Doctor, I am pregnant. The man who is responsible for the pregnancy wants me to abort it. Doctor, regard me now as your daughter who died. Tell me; convince me with reasons why I should not have an abortion.

DOCTOR: (*pensively*). I could have saved my Stella's life if I had been a better person. She knew I lived by carrying out abortions. She had to go through many herself. I never performed any on her, but anytime I discovered she'd had another one, she would simply laugh it off and say "Daddy, you earn your living by it, don't pretend you are a saint". What I could not achieve with my daughter, maybe I can achieve with you and maybe my conscience would finally come to rest. I will tell you what I don't tell my other patients- the dangers of abortion (*pulls her up and leads her to her seat*).

NIKE: Thank you Doctor.

DOCTOR: You see, many doctors can be very selfish; they keep the truth from the poor abortion seeker who has to undergo the horror and face future consequences. A lot of physical complications occur during induced abortion because the neck of the womb is tightly closed during pregnancy in order to protect the fetus. Forcing it open causes damage.

NIKE: Oh my God.

DOCTOR: Also, because the abortionist operates blindly, wrong manipulation of instruments can be very deadly. The uterus could be perforated, hemorrhage could result, and other internal organs may be destroyed. This can lead to sterility, miscarriages, and like I mentioned earlier, ectopic pregnancies.

NIKE: But people know about this and still continue with it?

DOCTOR: Yes. People are more concerned with immediate matters at the expense of future considerations. You see, recent researches have revealed that the risk of breast cancer is doubled among women who abort their first pregnancy. A high incidence of cervical cancer has also been found among women who abort. This is due to the fact that early in pregnancy, the breasts and uterus undergo rapid growth and change. The disruption of these changes before their completion renders the cells susceptible to 'neoplastic stimuli' or in layman's language, hastens the growth of cells that are already malignant.

NIKE: Doctor, you don't have to go on. I am convinced. I will not abort this pregnancy.

DOCTOR: Thank you very much my daughter, for giving me this opportunity to do one good turn in my life. From now onwards, no abortion shall be done at my clinic.

NIKE: Thank you for opening my eyes too. I know if I abort this pregnancy and in future I am not able to have any child for Chief, he might decide to take another wife. And if I have cancer, his already shaky love will completely fly out of the window.

DOCTOR: (*shakes his head in doubt*). Em, like I told you, you remind me of my dead daughter. She is dead, but you are alive. I would be failing in my paternal duty if it was Stella standing there and I refused to tell her this (*pauses*). However, I do not know how you will take it.

NIKE: (*resigned*). Well, I think today is meant to be my blow-collecting day. Before you arrived, my parents came in and disowned me. Chief came in and I saw him for what he really is- a mean and selfish man. What else can be more horrible than these?

DOCTOR: Then, let me give it to you straight. Chief will not marry you, and he never had any plan to do so.

NIKE: I can't believe this.

DOCTOR: This is what he usually promises to all his girlfriends. But you see, he is not really rich. The riches belong to his wife. She is the one that brought the business up. Her husband is actually her employee. She married him as a poor penniless clerk. She knows about his small escapades, she even knows about this love nest. If he attempts to marry another wife or even have a child by another woman, that would be the end of his marriage. He will never allow any woman to have his child except the woman happens to be richer than his wife. Actually, his wife is expecting their fourth child now.

NIKE: (*panicking*). Doctor, can all these be true?

DOCTOR: I do not have any cause whatsoever to lie to you.

NIKE: What shall I do then? Shall I run away before he comes?

DOCTOR: That will not be a good idea. If you do that, he is capable of coming to look for you and bumping you off.

NIKE: Oh, I am dead. Cursed be the day when I agreed to follow those girls to the party instead of going to listen to the lecture.

DOCTOR: Experience is the best teacher, and you did not have that.

NIKE: So, what should I do now?

DOCTOR: (*ponders awhile*). What I'll advise you to do is this: when he comes, pretend that you have had the abortion, and that you want to break the relationship. Then, go and hide yourself somewhere, have your child, and if you want to have the baby adopted, I can help you get a good home for him or her.

NIKE: I can't ever part with my baby. If I have to beg by the roadside to sustain both of us, I'll do it. My problem now is that I have nowhere to go. My parents have disowned me, and I can't go back to my room on the campus. Where can I go?

DOCTOR: I don't know. I really don't know. There is a limit to what I can do for you because if Chief traces you back to me, there will be trouble (*pauses*). Do you have a bank account?

NIKE: No. I don't have a dime to my name. The best I can do is to take all the things that Chief bought for me - clothes, jewelries and all. I'll sell them, rent a room for myself off-campus and see myself through this session with that. I'll then take one session off and get a job to enable me look after my baby.

DOCTOR: I see.

NIKE: I'll also apply for a scholarship; maybe I'll be lucky to get one. You see, I am a medical student at the university.

DOCTOR: Chief told me about that. Well I wish you the best of luck. I'll try and do as much as I can without implicating myself. When Chief pays me for this abortion, I'll send you a cheque. I will send it to your department. What is your full name?

NIKE: Nike Adedara.

DOCTOR: Good. I wish you the best of luck (*they shake hands and he exits*). Bye.

NIKE: (*Nike paces up and down*). So this is what I reap for my foolishness? God, please help me to get out of this alive (*she looks round the room*). My nest, you don't feel like a nest anymore, you feel more like a cage (*she exits into the bedroom*).

Blackout

Scene 2

Chief enters, singing a ditty. He is obviously drunk.

CHIEF: (*singing*). Ibi a ba ja'ye de, aye a mo pe a je'un …[18]

NIKE: (*comes in from the bedroom*). Ah Chief, what is the matter?

CHIEF: What do you mean? I am in this world to enjoy myself and nothing more. Come, come and sit beside me.

NIKE: (impassively). You have been away from this house for two days now. Where have you been?

CHIEF: Are you now trying to monitor my movement? I refuse to be tied to any woman's apron strings. I said come and sit beside me (*stands up and attempts to embrace Nike, but she pushes him away*).

NIKE: You are drunk and you know I can't stand the smell when you drink.

CHIEF: (*staggering*). You are stupid, you this foolish girl. Simply because I brought you out of the doldrums of poverty and established you in this beautiful and cushy house, you are beginning to have an over-inflated image of yourself. By the way, I hope you have had the abortion?

NIKE: (*No answer*).

CHIEF: Answer me, damn you. Have you done the abortion?

NIKE: (*tonelessly*). Yes.

CHIEF: (*happy*). Good. That's my girl (*attempts to embrace her, but she moves away*). Tomorrow, we'll go and obtain your passport and we'll start making arrangements for our trip to America. You know one reason why I love you? It is because you are so obedient and so loving.

NIKE: (*disgusted*). Chief, I want us to bring this affair to an end. You know you cannot marry me. I am tired of this farce. I want us to forget about each other and go our separate ways.

CHIEF: What the hell are you talking about? No girl tells me when to end an affair. I call the shots and I am still in love with you, so forget all about breaking up.

NIKE: Chief, I am serious about this. I have already packed my things. I will leave first thing tomorrow morning. It's been nice staying with you. You have helped me a lot and I appreciate it. But I have to leave.

CHIEF: Did I hear you say you have packed your things? If I remember correctly, you walked into this house with only one iro and buba on your back, and that is the only thing you will walk out with if you insist on going.

NIKE: Chief, you don't mean that, do you?

CHIEF: If another man has been toasting you, you can go and meet him in your one iro and buba, and he can jolly well buy you books for your course. But as far as I am concerned, you can even get out tonight. Go inside and change into your wretched clothes and get the hell out of my house (*she goes inside to change. Chief pours himself another drink*). That is the problem with all these village girls. When you civilize them, they want to get over-civilized. Nonsense (*projects his voice so that Nike would hear him*). If not that I don't want to be wicked, I'll charge you for the food you have been eating for the past three months and other expenses. It's only that I am a very good man. (*Nike comes out dressed*). Now, get out of my sight and never darken my doorsteps again. Asewo,[19] prostitute.

NIKE: (*stops and turns*). You are calling me a prostitute? You will certainly regret that.

CHIEF: (*screams*). You can still talk? Get out before I throw you out.

Blackout

PART THREE

Scene 1

A very dingy looking room. A rickety-looking table and chair. In a corner of the room are two buckets, a stove and some plates. Nike is sleeping on a mat spread on the floor. Dupe knocks and enters.

DUPE: (*looking worried*). Nike, I hope you are all right. I didn't see you at the department today, so I know something must be wrong. I know you don't joke with your lectures.

NIKE: Good afternoon Dupe (*she sits up and reveals her advanced stage of pregnancy*). The spirit is willing, but the flesh is weak. I tried to get up and come to the campus, but my body refused to cooperate.

DUPE: Have you been to the hospital?

NIKE: No, but I am feeling much better. Really, it wasn't anything major. You see, I am no longer strong enough to trek from the quarters to the campus and I did not have the bus fare.

DUPE: What a pity. You should have told me yesterday.

NIKE: Also, all the clothes I brought from the village are now so tight. It is only the famous or infamous iro and buba that I am still able to manage, and I am so sick and tired of it now.

DUPE: Don't worry; better days are ahead of you. But I wish you had damned the consequences and come back to our room. At least, it is an easy walking distance to the department.

NIKE: No way, Dupe. I cannot face Deola and Lanre in my shame. Let me just suffer it out here, licking my wounds in private. I will do my possible best to pass my exams so that I will not be advised to withdraw. Then I will go and work for a session to take care of my baby and try to save something. I have also applied for that scholarship you advised me to. The major problem is how to get over the rest of the three months that remain in this session. This abject penury is frustrating.

DUPE: Cheer up. You have been managing very well. Having seen you thus far, God will surely see you to the end.

NIKE: Amen. Oh, how bad of me, I have not even offered you a drink. Sorry, it can only be plain, honest-to-God water (*they both laugh as she goes to get the water*).

DUPE: (*opening her handbag*). You have a letter. I picked it up for you from the departmental office.

NIKE: (*pouring water into cups*). It is likely to be from my siblings in the village. They have been communicating with me surreptitiously (*coming back with the water*). My father's heart is still hardened. He was badly hit and the wound is still fresh.

DUPE: That is quite understandable.

NIKE: My mother is missing me as much as I'm missing her, but she dares not make any move because of my father.

DUPE: I understand how they feel. By God's grace, everything will fall into shape later.

NIKE: I strongly hope so (*sets the water down for Dupe and takes a cup for herself*).

DUPE: Thanks. Anyway, I don't think this letter is from your siblings. The address is typewritten. Here, (*hands the letter to Nike*) open it and let's see.

NIKE: (*takes it and turns it round and round*). Eh, could it be from the scholarship board?

DUPE: (*curious and impatient*). Oh, how can we know until you open it?

NIKE: (*opens it*). There is a cheque enclosed in it (*examines the cheque*). Twenty Thousand Naira! Ah, who could have sent me such a staggering sum of money?

DUPE: Why not read the letter and find out?

NIKE: (*she quickly scans through the letter*). Oh, it is from Dr. Dagunduro. He says Chief Agbabiaka has paid him for the abortion he was supposed to have performed on me. Just imagine that! Paying Twenty Thousand Naira for an abortion, yet, he sent me out without a kobo[20] to my name.

DUPE: You have had three months to get over the rough treatment you experienced at the hands of this man. I hope you will not allow bitterness to remain in your system.

NIKE: I can't help smarting about it from time to time.

DUPE: You should forget about the past and focus your attention on the future. Whatever would not contribute positively to that future-both your baby's and yours, forget about it. Now, this money, how do you plan to spend it?

NIKE: I've been thinking about it, even before the money arrived. How I have planned and strategised on how I'm going to spend the money, (*laughs*) although I never thought it would be as much as this.

DUPE: So what are your plans for the money?

NIKE: I think I'll buy two maternity gowns and I'll spend the rest on books. What do you think?

DUPE: (*ruminates*). The maternity gowns are necessary. But I think you have been managing quite well with library books and the ones you've been borrowing. I think you should rather think in terms of something that would cause the money to multiply.

NIKE: Is that possible?

DUPE: Yes. You live in the staff quarters, (*smiles*) not minding that you occupy the servants' section. You can start a small business selling things that are not easily obtainable in the quarters such as provisions, foodstuff and some other essential things.

NIKE: (*excited*). Oh!

DUPE: People who may not have time to dash to the market will come and buy from you.

NIKE: My dear friend, I thank you very much. You are a friend indeed because you have proved to be a friend in my time of need. I never thought about this before. When I'm going out for lectures or to the library, I'm sure my neighbors would be very willing to help me.

DUPE: Yes, I thought about that too.

NIKE: You see, I was afraid. I have been thinking about how I would buy nappies, cloths, feeders and so on, for my baby. Last week, on my way from the antenatal clinic, I stopped at the shopping mall to price baby things. I came back home and wept. The things are so expensive and so out of my reach. But with this new plan, my hope is renewed.

DUPE: Oh, you don't have to worry about baby things. I am planning a baby shower for you. We have a committee that takes care of such things in our church. I told them about you. I hope you will not mind that some of the things are not very new?

NIKE: (*becoming emotional*). Dupe, you must be an angel! I don't care whether they are new or not. This is very thoughtful of you. I am indeed very grateful. I don't know how to thank you. This is too much for me (*begins to cry*).

DUPE: (*moves to console her*). Please, stop crying. You know our people believe that if a woman cries too much during pregnancy, she will give birth to a cry-cry baby (*they both laugh*).

Blackout

Scene 2

Set, the same as in the previous scene, but there is an addition of a table on which bowls of foodstuff are displayed. A young man with a traveling bag walks onto the stage. The young man is Tayo Jackson.

TAYO: (*lifts his voice in greetings*). Good afternoon, is anybody at home?

NEIGHBOR: (*rushes out*). Good afternoon. What can I do for you? We have gari[21], rice and beans. Which one do you want to buy?

TAYO: Actually, I don't want to buy anything. I am looking for Nike Adedara.

NEIGHBOR: Aunty Nike is not yet back from lectures. Are you her brother?

TAYO: No. I am her friend. Can I wait for her?

NEIGHBOR: Yes, you can (*gives him a seat*). Please sit down here. I am working inside the house. I hope you don't mind. She will soon be back.

TAYO: Oh, I don't mind. Thank you very much (*She goes. Tayo sits down. After some time, he looks at his wristwatch and starts pacing up and down*). I might as well walk round the neighborhood and see what it is like while I am waiting (*he goes out*).

(*Nike enters in her new maternity gown*).

NIKE: (*calls out*). Mama Femi, I'm back.

NEIGHBOR: (*responding from inside*). Welcome. Have you seen your visitor?

NIKE: Visitor? Where is the visitor?

TAYO: (*coming onto the stage behind Nike*). I am here.

NIKE: Tayo, Tayo Jackson.

TAYO: In person! It's so nice to see you again.

43

NIKE: (*agitated*). But I wrote you that you shouldn't come.

TAYO: (*smiling*). Will you invite me in or are we going to stay here all day?

NIKE: I can't invite you in there. The place is horrible.

TAYO: You live there don't you? If you do, it will be heavenly I'm sure.

NIKE: (*shrugging her shoulders*). You've asked for it. Come in (*they enter the room*). Sit down. Be careful though, that chair is very rickety (*he sits on the chair while she sits on the mat*).

TAYO: Thank you.

NIKE: Tayo, why have you come? I wanted you to always remember me as that innocent girl you once knew. I didn't want you to see me in this shameful state.

TAYO: You are not being fair to me. What are friends for? You think I am a fair weather friend? I'll be a bad kind of friend if I am not there when you need a shoulder to weep on.

NIKE: I messed up. I really messed up my life. Many eyes were on me, expecting me to perform wonders, and I messed up.

TAYO: Don't torment yourself with such thoughts. You are a human being, and to err is human.

NIKE: Then you can call me super-human because I have super-erred.

TAYO: In this type of environment, how many people, who are fresh from a village, would not be confused and miss a step? You were young and innocent and that devil of a man took advantage of you. We all make mistakes at one point or the other in our lives.

NIKE: This one is a mega-mistake.

TAYO: The most important thing is for us to acknowledge that we have made a mistake and to desist from such a wrong action. If we fail to admit that we are making a mistake and die in our sin, then it will be a great tragedy.

NIKE: Tayo, thank you so much. It is such a big relief to see a face from my past. You know my parents have disowned me. I don't know how I'm going to reconcile with them. I really want to. It makes me very unhappy anytime I think about the strain in our relationship.

TAYO: I've just finished my exams, so I'll be going to the village today.

NIKE: Oh, selfish me! I've not even asked about your academics and your family.

TAYO: My parents and siblings are fine, and I am very optimistic about getting straight 'A's in all my papers.

NIKE: That's wonderful. I hope you enjoyed your first session in the university?

TAYO: Yes I did. Although I would have enjoyed it more if you had replied my letters. I was so anxious about you. When I went to the village for the semester break, I went to your house.

NIKE: You did? What did my parents say?

TAYO: When your mother saw me, she burst into tears and my heart almost flew out of my mouth. I feared the worst until she told me all that happened to you. That was when I wrote the last letter, which you replied forbidding me to come.

NIKE: What did my father say?

TAYO: He didn't say anything. He just walked out of the house. He couldn't bring himself to say anything to me. I will be going to the village today. I will gather the elders together and we will go and speak to your father. God willing, he will change his mind. I know he loves you very much.

NIKE: Yes, that is why he took it so badly.

TAYO: So how have you been faring- financially, physically, academically and so on?

NIKE: Hm, academically, I am not doing badly, although if I were to be my old self, I would have been performing better. I applied for a scholarship which I would really appreciate having. It is for the best student in the Faculty. The old me would be confident of winning it, but now I know of a certainty that I cannot get it. I have applied for another one that is not worth much. It is for less-privileged students. The outcome of the application will depend on the second semester results. I am starting my exams tomorrow.

TAYO: You seem to be underestimating yourself.

NIKE: I don't think so. Anyway, if I can win this other one, with the small yield that I realize rom my business, I will be able to take care of my baby and myself.

TAYO: (*rises up*). So you are the owner of that business outside there. You see, when I heard about your travails, I said to myself "my Nike will not cave in under the load of her trials. She will definitely rise to the occasion" and you did. I am proud of you my girl. I am glad that you did not abort that pregnancy.

NIKE: I am glad too. At least, I am alive and well, and I have a bright hope for the future. My life is not a bed of roses, but I have great faith that I will survive. People have rallied round me. Come and see, people that are absolute strangers gave me wonderful things for my baby … (*they move to examine the contents of a big bag*).

Blackout

Scene 3

Set, the same as in the previous scene except for the addition of a mattress placed on the mat, two easy chairs, a baby cot and Nike holding a baby.

NIKE: (*changing the baby's nappy and singing*). Baby, baby, my darling baby, there's no other baby as sweet as you (*knock on the door*). Come in (*Dupe enters*).

DUPE: Hello little mummy. How are you and your baby?

NIKE: Dupe good morning. We are both fine, thank you.

DUPE: You are handling him in a very professional way. You seem to have some experience.

NIKE: Yes. Remember I am the first child of a family of six. I helped my mother to bring up all my younger siblings.

DUPE: Oh, good for you. The experience is now paying off.

NIKE: Yes, but I wish I could have my mother's help and advice at this time. That would have been very useful.

DUPE: Does she know you have put to bed?

NIKE: Yes, I wrote to my parents. I hope the baby will serve as a magnet to draw them here. After all, it is their first grandchild, although years too early.

DUPE: We thank God for the safe delivery and everything.

NIKE: Well, I am not complaining. God has been good.

VOICE: Hey, who's there?

NIKE: Dupe, please help me attend to that person. Maybe she wants to buy something.

DUPE: (*goes outside*). Good morning madam. What can I do for you?

MRS. AGBA.: (*gorgeously dressed*). Are you Nike Adedara?

DUPE: No. She is inside.

MRS. AGBA.: I want to see her.

DUPE: Come in madam (*they both enter*).

NIKE: Good morning ma.

DUPE: How are you? So this is your baby?

NIKE: Yes madam, but I don't think I know you ma.

MRS. AGBA.: Certainly not. But you know somebody that is very close to me. I am Mrs. Agbabiaka.

NIKE: Oh no!

MRS. AGBA.: Oh yes. I am Chief Agbabiaka's wife.

NIKE: I am sorry.

MRS. AGBA.: You don't have to be. I knew all about your little affair and how he outsmarted you and threw you out.

NIKE: Well there is nothing between us anymore. There wouldn't have been anything between us in the first place if I knew he had a wife.

MRS. AGBA.: Yes, you were quite gullible. What a shame. You look quite intelligent to me. Anyway, I know he gave you a raw deal. You are the first woman who would actually have a child for him.

NIKE: I am sorry.

MRS. AGBA.: I can see you are not a mercenary at heart. If it is any comfort to you, I have withdrawn the entire financial succor I granted him in the past. He is now on a clerk's salary. He won't be able to mislead any other young innocent girl on a clerk's pay.

NIKE: I am very sorry that I caused a breach between you.

MRS. AGBA.: Oh that's all right. I have a small request for you.

NIKE: What is that ma?

MRS. AGBA.: I know you must have heard that I have four girls already. You have a boy for my husband, but you don't have the financial capability to bring him up the way he deserves. I want you to hand him over to me, and you shall be adequately compensated.

NIKE: Did I hear you right madam?

MRS. AGBA.: Yes, you are still very young and a baby cannot be anything but a liability to you. Think of what you can do with one million Naira.

NIKE: One million Naira?

MRS. AGBA.: Yes, that is the amount I am offering you to hand over my husband's baby and you will fade out of our lives. You will find your own husband and have other children later in life, I'm sure.

NIKE: I thank you very much madam. You are very magnanimous indeed.

MRS. AGBA.: Oh, it's nothing really. Anybody in my position would do the same.

NIKE: Things are really very hard for me at the moment. You can see the state of my room. I am still a student, sponsoring myself through school.

MRS. AGBA.: (*smugly*). The one million would come in handy.

NIKE: Things are very hard for me indeed (*suddenly turns ferocious*). But all these notwithstanding, my child is my child and he is not for sale. I will not sell him for a mess of pottage.

MRS. AGBA.: What? You cannot afford this unnecessary pride and arrogance.

NIKE: I know that things will be very tough, but God will see me through.

MRS. AGBA.: Okay. Let us strike a compromise. I will increase the money to two million Naira, and you can still be seeing the child from time to time, maybe once in five years or so.

NIKE: Thank you very much for calling madam. It has been nice meeting you.

MRS. AGBA.: So you know how to be insolent too. Insolence and poverty are strange bedfellows. Anyway, when you come to your senses, give me a call. You know my phone number?

NIKE: I do not care a hoot about your phone number.

MRS. AGBA.: (*laughs sardonically*). My new office is now in the place that used to be your love nest. You still remember the phone number don't you? (*she goes*).

NIKE: (*fuming*). What effrontery? What insolence? I think it is a sin to be rich. (*Shouts after her*). You think money can do everything for you? Just imagine the cheek, to hand over my child. Indeed, what a cheek!

DUPE: Calm down. She has gone. Don't mind her.

NIKE: How do I know she will not arrange to have my son kidnapped?

DUPE: Don't worry. We will go and inform the police.

NIKE: Let us go immediately. We mustn't leave anything to chance. I don't trust these people. They are criminals.

DUPE: Calm down. Everything will be taken care of.

FRIEND: (*bursts in without knocking*). Congratulations Nike. Have you heard?

NIKE: Heard what? What is that?

FRIEND: Can't you guess?

NIKE: (*irritably*). Look, I am in no mood for a guessing game. You either tell me or keep it. Come, Dupe, let us go.

FRIEND: Why are you in such a bad mood? Anyway, congratulations, the scholarship list is out and you won the Faculty scholarship.

NIKE: Will you get out of here? Today is not April 1. You can't make a fool out of me.

FRIEND: But I mean it. Isn't your name Nike Adedara, registration number 36951?

NIKE: So what?

FRIEND: Okay, let us go and check it together.

NIKE: Dupe, please hold my baby while I go.

FRIEND: (*they both rush out leaving Dupe with the baby*). Let's go.

DUPE: (*flustered*). What if he starts crying? This is serious. I can't remember any lullaby (*while trying to sort herself out with the baby, somebody knocks on the door*). Come in.

Tayo Jackson enters with Nike's parents.

TAYO: Greetings, we are here to see Nike. These are her parents.

DUPE: Welcome sir, welcome ma. I'm so glad to see you all.

TAYO: Thank you. Where is Nike?

DUPE: She went to the Faculty to check her scholarship results.

MOTHER: (*excitedly*). Is this my grandson? (*she carries him*). My very first grandchild! My God, I thank you for giving me this privilege.

DUPE: I am so glad that you have finally forgiven Nike. To err is human, to forgive, divine.

FATHER: Actually, it was my pride that prevented me from extending the olive branch to her since all these days. I feel so bad that she had to suffer alone for so long.

TAYO: Papa, forget about all that. All is well that ends well.

NIKE: (*rushes in*). It is true. I won. I won the scholarship (*embraces both her parents*). Oh my father, my mother! Tayo, you did it, you've given me my family again.

FATHER: My daughter.

MOTHER: Adenike.

NIKE: Kneeling down. I have learnt my lesson in a bitter way. Please forgive me.

FATHER: (*pulls her up*). You are forgiven. From now on, let there always be openness between us. Don't ever hide your problems from us again.

MOTHER: Nike, I want you to know that it could have been worse. Many girls have lost their lives in this kind of mess.

FATHER: Yes. Last month, we read about the death of one female undergraduate whose ritual murder was perpetrated by her so-called sugar daddy. The rogue of a man is in police net right now, but will that bring the girl back to life?

MOTHER: Another girl has been missing now for the past nine months. When she left her room, she told her roommates that she was going out with her sugar daddy. The man denied having seen her. Nobody knows her fate.

FATHER: How many cases of fatalities through abortion do we want to mention. We just thank God that you got off as lightly as this and I hope you have learnt your lesson.

NIKE: Father, indeed, I have learnt my lesson. I will never go back to my vomit like the proverbial dog.

Mother, father and Nike hug.

TAYO: See the baby nestling so comfortably in Mama's arms.

NIKE: Yes. He is confident that he is enclosed within the cage of our love. We shall never allow evil to come near him.

FATHER: Neither shall we allow him to run off and go astray. What name do you call him?

NIKE: I call him Love.

Blackout

EPILOGUE

Back to the assembly hall. Nike Adagunodo in her role as storyteller.

ADAGUNODO: So, my dear girls, it has not been easy. My life has not been a bed of roses. Like my mother said, it could have been worse. I have been luckier than most girls who went astray. That is why I do not wish you to go astray. I passed through medical school and my people rallied round me. I am now a medical doctor today, by the grace of God (*turns to Busola*). You wonder where I met Mr. Adagunodo? Well, Tayo Jackson decided to drop his foreign name and he took on his family name, Adagunodo. He saw that the brief mistake in my life did not become a permanent vice. He saw that from then on, I kept myself pure. He proposed marriage to me and I accepted. We got married twenty years ago. Our son, Love, is now a graduate. His younger ones are doing quite well too. Is there anyone here who has made a mistake? You feel you have messed your life real bad? It is not too late. Arise with determination that your tomorrow will be better. Refuse to be defeated. Refuse to bow. Never you ensnare yourself in a cage as you search for a nest. Arise everybody, let us sing this song together: Break Forth (as the song starts, *Busola moves towards Mrs. Adagunodo. They embrace*).

SONG: (*everybody sings*).
Break forth
Yes, break forth into joy
Break all chains, break all fetters
Don't seek a nest to nestle in all day long
Don't be a sluggard, don't laze away
Don't be content to stay in a cage
While you may live in a nest of your own making
Break out, break forth.

Let your light shine
Arise, shine

For your light has come
Arise, shine
Out of the ashes of your shame
Out of the shame of your disgrace
Take your life in your hands
The only person that can destroy you is yourself
Arise, shine, shine, yes, shine
For your light has come
Shine, shine, shine, yes shine!

Blackout

THE END

GLOSSARY

[1]Adenike, welcome
Paragon College, Adenike greets you
We salute you Adenike
Wife of Adagunodo
A good wife in the home of her husband
The accomplished physician that cures a multitude of sicknesses
Adenike we salute you
Hands of gold, feet of gold
Adenike step softly and elegantly, all eyes are on you
Do step softly and elegantly, all eyes are on you
Adenike step softly and elegantly
Child of a celebrity, wife of a celebrity
 you are also a celebrity in your own right
There is no pauper in your lineage
All members of your family tree are rich
People, come and watch our play
People come and watch our performance
Who has assembled us here?
It is Nike Adagunodo
What is the reason for our assembly?
Nike Adagunodo is the reason
Long may you lead us, wife of Adagunodo
What is that sound I hear in the sky?
I look up and behold a jet
It is Nike Adagunodo
Her conveyance is an airplane
Feet of gold must not trail in the dust
Nike Adagunodo
Carefully tread the ground, gently tread the ground
The best welcome for a visitor is "carefully tread the ground"
You are welcome.

[2] Aluta- Shortened form of the expression 'Aluta Continua, Victoria Acerta' roughly translated 'the struggle continues, victory is certain'. This is usually the rallying cry of students in institutions of higher learning in Nigeria whenever they are on the warpath, demonstrating against perceived injustices perpetrated by institutional authorities or the Nigerian government

[3] Anti-SAP Riots – SAP is acronym for Structural Adjustment Program. Nigeria operated this economic program during the Babangida regime (1985 – 1993). In June 1989 there was a public uprising of the masses to protest the economic woes experienced by the general populace. This led to a total breakdown of law and order, which resulted in the temporary closure of all government and private institutions to curb the attendant looting and vandalization.

[4] Bobo nice- Literally means 'the guy is just nice to me'. There are two types of men referred to in this way- sugar daddies who give girls expensive gifts and cash in exchange for an affair. But the girl deceives her friends that there is no amorous side to the relationship. The other type is the younger man who plies a girl with gifts but is too shy to declare his amorous intention.

[5] Serving- Every University and Polytechnic graduate in Nigeria, within a certain age group, is expected to serve in the National Youth Service Corps for a year after graduation. Corpers are posted to various states of the Federation apart from their natal states to work in various fields. They are also paid a small fraction of the usual pay for graduates. It is a service to the nation.

[6] Jambite- A fresher in a Nigerian university. The matriculation exam is organized by a body known as JAMB. Hence, a matriculant is popularly referred to as jambite.

[7] Oya- Yoruba word meaning it is time.

[8] Abi- Yoruba word, which in this context means 'or'.

[9] Na bobo and shakara- Pidgin English meaning pretence.

[10] October rush- Nigerian academic session starts in September. After the initial settling-in process, old male students begin aggressive courting of fresh female students in October.

[11] Sun gas'- A type of hairstyle popular in the 1970s with Nigerian women.

The hair is plaited in multiple spike forms with thread. It has now become obsolete with the prevalence of Western hairstyles.

[12] How you dey?- Pidgin English meaning 'How are you'?

[13] GPA- Grade Point Average. This is calculated for students at the end of every semester to indicate the cumulative grades obtained. It would eventually determine which class of degree the student graduates with.

[14] NCE- National Certificate of Education.

[15] Everyday no be Chrismas. Even lecturers dey take day-off- Pidgin English stating that It is not everyday that is Christmas or meant for celebration. In recognition of this need to set celebratory days apart, even lecturers sometimes take some days off from classes.

[16] Sprayed – The act of pasting the heads of dancers and musicians with currency notes in appreciation of their performances during celebrations.

[17] Iro and Buba- The traditional floppy-armed blouse associated with Yoruba women of Western Nigeria.

[18] Ibi a ba ja'ye de, aye a mo pe a je'un ...- A drunkard's ditty stating the singer's determination to enjoy life to its fullest.

[19] Asewo - Prostitute

[20] Kobo – The Nigerian currency is divided into units of Naira and Kobo, 1kobo being the smallest denomination. One hundred Kobo = One Naira.

[21] Gari – A staple Nigerian food made from cassava tubers.